MW01173954

SALLY RIDE

Gloria D. Miklowitz

Dominie Press, Inc.

Publisher: Raymond Yuen
Editor: Bob Rowland
Designer: Greg DiGenti
Photo Credits: Douglas Kirkland/Corbis (cover and Page 34); Bettmann/Corbis (pages 7, 20, and 26); and the National Aeronautics and Space Administration (Page 14)

Published by:

Dominie Press, Inc.

1949 Kellogg Avenue
Carlsbad, California 92008 USA

www.dominie.com

Paperback ISBN 0-7685-3046-6
Library Bound Edition ISBN 0-7685-3573-5
Printed in Singapore by PH Productions Pte Ltd
1 2 3 4 5 PH 07 06 05

Table of Contents

Chapter 1

Exploring the Universe

On the morning of June 18, 1983, Dr. Sally Ride won her place in history as the first American woman to be launched into space.

At 3:15 that morning, an alarm clock woke Sally for her date with history. It was still dark outside. In a few hours, she would leave Earth in a space shuttle with a crew of four other astronauts, all men.

As she prepared for the day's launch, Sally must have wondered what was in store. What would it be like blasting off from Earth? Floating around in zero gravity? Circling the world and seeing sunrises and sunsets sixteen times every twenty-four hours?

Four hours later, Sally Ride was launched into history aboard the space shuttle *Challenger*.

Sally Ride was born in Encino, California on May 26, 1951, the daughter of Dale and Carol Joyce Ride. Her father was a political science professor at Santa Monica Community College, and her mother was a teacher.

Sally Ride and the other crew members of the **Challenger** *make their way to their spacecraft on June 18, 1983*

Sally was surrounded by books at home, and her parents loved reading. She was given the freedom to explore. "We just let Sally and Bear (the nickname given to her younger sister, Karen) develop normally," said her father. The Rides "were not a normal family," according to Sally's friend,

Molly Tyson. "People ate dinner when they wanted, and they could have a whole dinner of nuts and cheese and crackers."

As a child, Sally loved sports. She was a natural athlete. Able to read at five, she yanked the sports section out of the newspaper before her father got to it.

An important world event occurred in 1957, when Sally was only seven. The Russians sent a female black-and-white fox terrier named Laika into space in a spacecraft called *Sputnik*. At the time, no one knew if living creatures could survive blasting off from Earth, and return alive. Laika died because the Russians weren't able to bring *Sputnik* back to Earth. It would be years before a human being could be launched safely into space. Sally was only a child at that time. She could not have imagined that one day she would be one of the fortunate few to travel into the vastness of space.

When Sally was ten, she took up tennis. By her teens, she was a nationally ranked tennis player. Billie Jean King considered her so good that she suggested she leave school and turn professional. Sally's tennis ability brought her a partial scholarship to the private Westlake School for Girls in Los Angeles.

Sally's interest in science began when she was eleven and received a telescope as a gift. With the inexpensive scope, she learned much about the skies above. A year later she received a chemistry set. But it was at Westlake that her interest in science blossomed. There, a former UCLA professor, Dr. Elizabeth Mommaerts, taught science and was particularly interested in space. The teacher's clear thinking, intelligence, and logic appealed to Sally, and they became good friends.

After high school, Sally entered Swarthmore College, in Swarthmore, Pennsylvania. She was planning to study astronomy, the scientific exploration of the universe. Sally left Swarthmore after three semesters because she missed California and transferred to Stanford University, in northern California. There she studied English and Physics. In 1973, she received two degrees, one in the arts and one in science.

Next she applied to graduate school at Stanford. Three years later, while finishing work for her doctorate in physics, she read an ad in the campus newspaper. The National Aeronautics and Space Administration (NASA) was looking for young scientists, men *and* women, to serve as specialists on future space flights. It was the first time women were included in the space program.

"Suddenly I knew that I wanted a chance to see the Earth and the stars from outer space," Sally later wrote. The day she saw the ad she mailed a postcard requesting an application.

Chapter 2

Launching the Space Race

Thousands of people responded to NASA's ad, seeking to become part of the space program. Some hoped to fly the spacecraft. Others wanted to be mission specialists—those who would help solve scientific problems. Of the almost 8,000 who applied, over 1,250 were women.

In October 1977 Sally learned that she was one of the finalists. She was flown to the Johnson Space Center in Houston, Texas, for physical and mental tests and an interview with the selection committee. Three months later, the results were in. Thirty-five individuals were chosen to be astronauts in training. Of those, six were women. Sally was one of the six. She was so excited, she exclaimed, "I'd like to go up (into space) tomorrow!"

Although Sally said she didn't know why she was chosen, her strong science background counted heavily. Also, she learned new things quickly and was resourceful. Those are important qualities for an astronaut.

To illustrate Sally's resourcefulness, her friend, Molly Tyson, told of the night the two of them were stranded on

Sally Ride undergoes training at the Johnson Space Center, in Houston, Texas

a dark California road. Sally's car had broken down because of a burst radiator hose. Sally immediately set about solving the problem. She found a roll of tape in the trunk and used it to repair the radiator hose. Then she found an old saucepan "rattling around in back" and went looking for water. In an hour they were back on the road.

Soon after receiving her doctorate, Sally reported to the Johnson Space Center for training. For the next three years, it was "back to school" to learn everything about the space shuttle and the experiments the crew would conduct in space.

The race to conquer space—a global contest between Russia and the United States—began seventeen years before Sally joined NASA. She was only ten when Russia launched a cosmonaut named Yuri Gagarin into space in April 1961. Less than a month later, on May 5, 1961, Alan Shepard became the first American to enter space. Though Shepard spent less than fifteen minutes in space aboard *Freedom 7*, his historic flight laid the groundwork for future U.S. space exploration. Ten years later, Shepard became the fifth man to walk on the moon. While he was on the moon, he played golf with a club he had carried onboard the lunar spacecraft of *Apollo 14*.

The earliest astronauts were like human guinea pigs. Would weightlessness affect their bones? Would radiation harm them? With each successful launch, greater feats seemed possible.

But could America land an astronaut on the moon and bring him back safely to Earth? This question was answered when Neil Armstrong became the first human to set foot on the moon. Armstrong was the commander of the first Apollo mission—*Apollo 11*—to land on the moon in July 1969. He received the Presidential Medal of Freedom and numerous international awards for his service on *Apollo 11*.

While Sally was still in high school, space probes were being sent up to explore other planets. Satellites launched into space sent back pictures and information about conditions on Earth. The rockets that carried those satellites were never used again.

By the time Sally was in college, a new kind of vehicle, called a shuttle, was in the works. It would be capable of carrying a crew of astronauts and a cargo of satellites and equipment into space. Part rocket, part spacecraft, and part aircraft, it could go into space and return to Earth, again and again.

This was the moment in history when Sally Ride entered NASA's space program. Men and women with strong science backgrounds—people who were creative, intelligent, resourceful, and healthy—were needed. Sally Ride displayed all of those qualities.

Chapter 3

Training for the *Challenger*

During Sally's second year of training, NASA informed her that she would be one of the crew members on the shuttle *Challenger*, for the seventh shuttle mission. "The third and last year of training was very intense," she said in a televised interview. She would be part of a crew of five. The other four were: Robert Crippen, commander; Frederick (Rick) Hauck, copilot; Dr. Norman Thagard; and John Fabian.

As flight engineer, Sally would sit behind the pilot and copilot during takeoff and landing to keep an eye on over 2,000 dials and blinking lights on the control panel. She had a checklist of things to do if anything went wrong. "There's an awful lot to watch up there, and we need a third pair of eyeballs," Crippen said.

During that third year, the crew prepared for the coming mission by taking part in practice launches, reentries, and landings. They also rehearsed everything they would need to do while they were in orbit.

Sally worked with the people who

Sally Ride communicates with Mission Control from the space shuttle Challenger

created the experiments carried by the mission. She needed to understand how the satellites should work. If anything went wrong during the flight, she would need to know how it could be fixed.

She and John Fabian were assigned to operate a fifty-foot robot arm that Sally helped design. It would be placed in the shuttle's cargo bay, a compartment at the rear of the shuttle that could be opened in space. The robot arm was designed to lift equipment in and out of the shuttle while it was in orbit.

In the last months before the flight, Sally became the contact person between Mission Control on the ground and shuttle crews 185 miles up in space. If the crew had a problem, scientists would work out a solution and Sally would guide the astronauts in fixing the problem.

With their flight date set, it became important for Sally and the *Challenger* crew to stay in good physical shape. She ran four to five miles a day—something she did when she was in college. "I can't say I like to run. I really don't," she told an interviewer. But she did it because she wanted to stay in shape.

Finally, after three years of intensive training, Sally and the crew of the *Challenger* were ready for the most important day of their lives—their journey into space.

Chapter 4

Liftoff!

It's four o'clock in the morning on June 18, 1983—three hours before launch. Dressed in their flight suits, Sally and the crew get last-minute instructions and eat a light breakfast. A van drives them to the launch pad nine miles away at the Kennedy Space Center in Cape Canaveral, Florida.

The space shuttle is thirty stories high. "We can hear it (the shuttle) hissing and gurgling as though it's alive," Sally wrote in *To Space and Back*, a children's book about the flight. The astronauts take an elevator 195 feet up to a level near the nose of the shuttle and walk into a small, white chamber. There, six technicians help them into escape harnesses and helmets and strap them into their seats. Because the shuttle is on its tail, they lie on their backs, facing the nose. In that position, it's hard to see anything out of the windows.

An hour before launch, they check everything. Then they wait. The technicians close the hatch and head for safety. A few miles away, thousands of Americans, some of whom have traveled long distances, are anxiously checking the sky.

Seven minutes before launch the shuttle begins to shudder. The astronauts close their helmets and begin breathing from their oxygen supply. Then, the shuttle quivers as its engines ready for blastoff.

10—9—8—7—6—5... The shuttle shakes and strains as the three launch engines light.

4—3—2—1... The rockets light. "The shuttle leaps off the launch pad in a cloud of steam and trail of fire. Our heads are rattling around inside our helmets," Sally wrote. "We can barely hear the voices from Mission Control in our headsets above the thunder of rockets and engines."

Two minutes later, the rockets burn out and fall away. The shuttle is suddenly quiet, and the ride is smooth as it streaks on toward space. The

Sally Ride poses with the other members of the space shuttle Challenger

launch engines, still attached to the shuttle, are hurtling them out of Earth's atmosphere. Six minutes from launch, they feel three times the normal gravity pressing them hard against their seats. "I find myself wishing we'd hurry up and get into orbit," Sally wrote.

Eight and a half minutes into the flight the engines cut off, and the gravity force pushing against them is gone. The empty fuel tank drops away and falls to Earth. They are in space, but only fifty miles up. A final boost by the shuttle's smaller space engines puts them into their final orbit, almost 200 miles above Earth.

Now it is very quiet, except for the hum of fans circulating air. They are traveling at five miles a second, orbiting around Earth once every ninety minutes. Earth looks like a big blue-and-white marble, and they can see mountain ranges and seas, cities and deserts.

Now they are feeling weightless, Sally says in her book. It's nothing like the simulated weightlessness they experienced on Earth. They begin somersaulting and playing, pushing against the walls to float or move up a stairway, and sitting on the ceiling.

Sally needs a water gun to wash herself and brush her teeth. With it she shoots water onto a cloth to wash, or into her mouth to brush her teeth and spit the water into a cloth.

The crew takes turns preparing meals. Each astronaut's tray is attached to the wall of the shuttle with Velcro. Packets of food are set in slots on the tray to hold them in place. Some foods, in plastic containers, have to be squirted with water, and then shaken and sipped through a straw.

Sally and the crew discover that weightless food is fun to play with. They chase jelly beans twirling around in the cabin, and push off walls to capture the floating beans in their mouths.

Everyone sleeps at the same time. Some float around. Others go into their sleeping bags, which are attached to a wall. Some sleep upside down on the ceiling. If something goes wrong, the computers will sound an alarm and Mission Control will call them.

Chapter 5

Mission Accomplished

An important part of the *Challenger* mission was to carry satellites into orbit and launch them at the right moment, in the right spot, and pointed in the right direction. Sally and John Fabian were in charge of operating the robot arm to move the satellites—some as small as a basketball, others as big as a bus—in or out of the cargo bay.

Sally's tasks included sending into space two communication satellites, running about forty scientific experiments, repairing equipment, and assisting the commander and pilot during the flight. Despite her busy schedule, she took time as often as possible to gaze out the windows. "You can see one thousand miles in any direction up there," she said. "You get to see several countries on Earth at once, only you don't see any borders."

The day before returning, the crew "cleaned up." They collected trays, pencils, and notebooks—everything that was loose—to store in drawers where they couldn't hurt anyone during reentry. Their seats had to be reattached so they could sit in them again. Their space suits and boots had to be found and put on. Finally, Sally and the crew strapped themselves into their seats, connected their helmets to the oxygen, and started the small engines to bring them back home.

Because of poor weather, the shuttle *Challenger* landed in California instead of Florida. Sally said she was amazed that, after six days of weightlessness, her body felt like lead and her heart beat much faster. For about fifteen minutes after landing, she felt dizzy and unsure of her balance. But soon she was ready to leave the shuttle and walk down the stairs to the runway. Because of the unexpected change in the landing site, only a small crowd had gathered. One sign read, "Herstory made today by Sally Ride."

Sally went into space once more, in 1984, and was preparing for a third trip when tragedy struck. On January 29, 1986 a seven-member crew launched aboard the *Challenger* space shuttle blew up seventy-three seconds after liftoff. All seven astronauts died. Sally was deeply affected because, "Those were the astronauts I entered the program with." She was appointed to a commission to investigate the disaster.

Since leaving her life as an astronaut, Sally has advised NASA on future space programs. She foresees astronauts returning to the moon and landing on Mars. Now a professor of space science at the University of California at San Diego, she is actively promoting educational programs that encourage women to go into the sciences. In June 2003, Sally was inducted into the U.S.

Sally Ride, after becoming the first American woman to be launched into space

Astronaut Hall of Fame, the first woman to be so honored.

"The thing that I'll remember most about the flight," Sally said, "is that it was fun. In fact, I'm sure it was the most fun that I will ever have in my life."

Glossary

Astronaut – a person who is trained to travel and perform tasks in space.

Copilot – a second pilot in an airplane or spacecraft who shares in the flying but is not in command.

Cosmonaut – an astronaut in the space programs of Russia and the former Soviet Union.

Doctorate – the highest college degree a person can earn.

Experiments – scientific tests.

Feats – accomplishments or achievements.

Guinea Pigs – people or animals used as the subjects of experiments.

Hatch – a door cut into an aircraft.

Herstory – history as it affects women; history made by women or from a woman's point of view.

Hurtling – moving or traveling at very high speed.

Launch – to send a rocket or satellite into space.

Mars – the fourth planet from the sun. (Earth is the third planet from the sun.)

Orbit – the path that an object follows around a planet.

Oxygen – a colorless, odorless gas that people and animals need in order to breathe.

Physics – the scientific study of energy, matter, and motion.

Radiation – energy in the form of rays or waves.

Reentries – return trips to Earth's atmosphere.

Resourceful – good at solving problems, especially under difficult circumstances.

Satellites – objects put into orbit around the Earth or other planets in order to send signals or relay information.

Scholarship – financial aid given to a student by a college or university to help with living expenses, study, or travel.

Simulated – an artificial condition made to feel like an actual experience.

Technician – a person who has a specialized skill.

Velcro – a trademarked name for a fastener consisting of a strip with a surface of tiny hooks that fasten to a second strip with a surface of tiny loops.